Out There?

MYSTERIOUS SIGNS

John Townsend

Raintree

www.raintreepublishers.co.uk

Visit our website to find out more information about **Raintree** books.

To order:
- ☎ Phone 44 (0) 1865 888113
- ▤ Send a fax to 44 (0) 1865 314091
- 💻 Visit the Raintree Bookshop at **www.raintreepublishers.co.uk** to browse our catalogue and order online.

First published in Great Britain by Raintree Publishers, Halley Court, Jordan Hill, Oxford OX2 8EJ, part of Harcourt Education Ltd. Raintree is a registered trademark of Harcourt Education Ltd.

Editorial: Charlotte Guillain and Isabel Thomas
Design: Michelle Lisseter and Bridge Creative Services Ltd
Picture Research: Maria Joannou and Kay Altwegg
Production: Jonathan Smith

Originated by Ambassador
Printed and bound in China and Hong Kong by South China

ISBN 1 844 43216 5
08 07 06 05 04
10 9 8 7 6 5 4 3 2 1

British Library Cataloguing in Publication Data
Townsend, John, 1924
Mysterious signs – (Out there)
1. Signs and symbols – Juvenile literature
2. Curiosities and wonders – Juvenile literature
3. Human-alien encounters – Juvenile literature
001.9'4

A full catalogue record for this book is available from the British Library.

Acknowledgements
Page 06 bott, Fortean Picture Library/; 06 top, Corbis/; 08 bott, Fortean Picture Library/; 08 top, Corbis/Christopher Cormack; 09, Fortean Picture Library/Terence Meaden; 10 top, Fortean Picture Library/F C Taylor; 10 bott, Fortean Picture Library/; 11, Weetabix Ltd/; 12–13, Rex Features/Steve Alexander; 12, British Film Institute/; 13, Buena Vista International/; 14–15, Lonely Planet/Chris Beall; 15, Photodisc/; 17 left, Fortean Picture Library/ Klaus Aarsleff; 16, Lonely Planet/; 18–19, Corbis/Yann Arthus-Bertrand; 18, Corbis/Angelo Hornak; 19, Alamy Images/; 20 right, Corbis/Roman Soumar; 20 left, Fortean Picture Library/; 21, Corbis/; 22–23, Corbis/Niall Benvie; 22, Photodisc/; 23, Corbis/Richard Nowitz; 25, /Rob Pilgrim; 24, Corbis/Hubert Stadler; 24–25, Fortean Picture Library/; 26–27, Corbis/Kevin Schafer; 26, Corbis/James Amos; 27, Corbis/Ric Ergenbright; 28–29, Fortean Picture Library/Dr Elmar Gruber; 28, Fortean Picture Library/ Klaus Aarsleff; 29, Corbis/Bill Ross; 30–31, Corbis/; 30, /Peter Evans; 31, /Peter Evans; 30–31, Photodisc/; 34–35, Corbis/Staffan Widstrand; 34, RSPCA Photo Library/; 36–37, Corbis/Danny Lehman; 36, Corbis/; 38 right, Corbis/Richard Cooke; 39, Corbis/Yann Arthus-Bertrand; 40–41, Corbis/Richard A. Cooke; 40, Fortean Picture Library/Klaus Aarsleff; 41, Corbis/Paul Souders; 42–43, Getty Images Taxi/; 42, Corbis/David Muench; 43, /John Miles; 44–45, Corbis/Charles O'Rear; 45, Science Photo Library/; 46 bott, Fortean Picture Library/Dazso Sternoczky/SUFOI; 46 top, Science Photo Library/; 47, Science Photo Library/; 49, Science Photo Library/; 48 left, Science Photo Library/US Geological Survey; 48–49, Photodisc/; 50, Photodisc/; 44, Ronald Grant Archive.

Cover photograph reproduced with permission of Corbis.

Every effort has been made to contact copyright holders of any material reproduced in this book. Any omissions will be rectified in subsequent printings if notice is given to the publishers.

CONTENTS

Any words appearing in the text in bold, **like this**, are explained in the Glossary. You can also look out for them in the Weird words box at the bottom of each page.

WHAT ON EARTH DO WE LOOK LIKE?

> If this is E.T. phoning home, I hope he uses someone else's corn field next time.

A UK farmer after strange signs appeared in his crops in 1990.

Our planet is full of secrets. These secrets have puzzled **mankind** for years yet little has ever been explained. Why do some places hold such strange powers? Can puzzles from the past help unravel some of the Earth's mysteries?

Eyes looking down from space may see far more than we ever will.

WEIRD WORDS

alien   from another world
mankind   human species over thousands of years

THE VIEW FROM ABOVE

People often see weird and mysterious things. Seeing these things from the ground is strange enough. But when we look down on the Earth from the sky we can see even more amazing sights.

ALIEN LIFE?

Perhaps the strange marks we can see on the Earth are signs that **aliens** once visited our planet. They could be signs that others have been here before us. If so, who? Why did they leave these marks and what do they mean?

HIDDEN POWERS

Science cannot explain all of the Earth's mysteries. Even though we now understand some of the signs we once thought were alien, there are still unanswered questions. What powers does our planet hold? What forces are at work?

There may be much more to these mysteries than meets the eye.

FIND OUT LATER...

What made these signs in the fields?

Is this a runway for alien spacecraft?

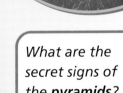

*What are the secret signs of the **pyramids**?*

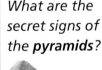

pyramid   large stone monument with sloping sides and a point

SIGNS AND WONDERS

STRANGE SHAPES

Crop circles come in all shapes and sizes: keys or claws, weird insects, stars in space...

Crop circles are flattened areas in cornfields. They often appear overnight in the shape of circles or other designs. But what makes them? Are they:

- the result of the weather?
- jokes made by people?
- the marks of **aliens**? Perhaps there are other secrets behind these circles. They may be more mysterious than we think.

Many crop markings are in the shape of keys.

Could humans really create designs like this at night, without anyone noticing?

WEIRD WORDS   fraction   just a small part of the total
sacred   special in a religious way

WEIRD PATTERNS

Strange shapes in crops have puzzled us for hundreds of years. They have only been studied in detail in the last 30 years. Since we have been able to take photos from the sky, we have begun to see them better and wonder more about them.

Ireland

United Kingdom

Wiltshire

London

WHAT ON EARTH ARE THEY?

Some circles show amazing designs. Are they **sacred symbols**? Are they trying to tell us something? Are there strange forces at work? There are plenty of ideas out there as to what the patterns really are.

Thousands of crop circles have appeared in Wiltshire, UK, in the last 50 years.

WHERE ON EARTH ARE THEY?

You can often see these strange designs in cornfields. But the patterns are not only found in fields of crops. You can also see them in grass, sand, soil, snow and ice. Sometimes they appear in leaves on trees.

In fact, they may be all around us but we cannot always see them. We may see only a **fraction** of these strange 'fingerprints'.

HOT SPOTS

Crop circles seem to 'crop up' all over the world. But they appear in some areas more often than others. Wiltshire in England is one of the hottest spots for crop circles every year.

Fast fact

Crop circles have appeared in Australia, Canada, Israel, Japan, South Africa, the UK, the USA and about 40 other countries.

- The earliest crop circle on record is thought to have been in Assen, Holland in 1590.

- The largest crop circle filled a whole field – over 330 metres across.

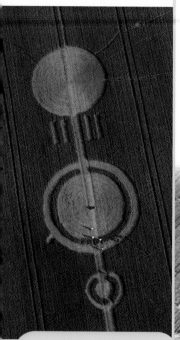

In some crop circles, microphones have stopped working properly.

DESIGN

The amazing thing about these circles is their design. They are all different and some are very **complex**. It is hard to believe they just happen by chance. Someone must have planned each part. Every line seems to fit and every little shape plays its part in the whole design. The full effect is hard to see from the ground.

WHIRLWINDS

Some scientists think the weather may play a part in making the circles. Perhaps the flow of air over hills may make mini-whirlwinds. These winds could be charged with electricity. This could explain why some people have seen lights or heard humming around crop circles.

Crop circles have to be seen from above.

WEIRD WORDS

complex   very complicated and detailed
magnetic   pulling force

REED CIRCLES

Although strange circles may have appeared long ago, they have only been **examined** in recent years. In Australia, people only began to notice strange shapes in swamps in the 1960s. These **reed** circles appeared in the swamps near Tully in Queensland. Then people saw patterns in fields nearby.

FOREST CIRCLES

Hundreds of giant forest circles have appeared in the north of Canada. They can only be seen from the air and some are over 2 kilometres (1.25 miles) across. One idea is that electrical energy inside the Earth may make the trees grow in this way. But no one knows for sure what is really behind the patterns.

A SURGE OF POWER?

We have always known that the Earth has some amazing forces:

- electrical energy
- **magnetic** fields
- **radiation**.

Perhaps they may explain some crop patterns. We are still finding out how these forces affect us and our planet.

Could mini-whirlwinds make crop circles?

radiation   invisible waves of energy that can be harmful in high doses

MARKS BY HUMAN HANDS

Strange air currents cannot explain how all crop circles **form**. Many people think that they are man-made. Crop circles often appear in the early morning in **remote** places. We now know that many crop circles are made by people. Some are done as a **hoax**. Others are done as a form of crop art.

This pattern seems too **complex** to be a hoax.

MYSTERY

Can all crop circles be made by humans overnight? Experts do not know how this strange design was made on Milk Hill, Wiltshire, England in 2001. It had 409 circles and was nearly 300 metres across. That would take many people all day to make.

Humans can make crop circles, but it takes a long time.

Experts have studied bent stalks and soil inside crop circles. Sometimes they find higher **magnetic** readings inside the circles than outside. It is still hard to prove if humans have made the pattern or if it is something else.

form   to be made and come into shape
hoax   joke, trick or something that is not real

HOAX

So how do you make a crop circle? The tools are simple: a **stake,** a rope, some boards and a few people.

In 1978, Doug Bower and his friends began the craze of making crop circles. Doug had lived in Australia when circles first appeared in Queensland. Stories spread about **alien** spacecraft landing in the area. Doug had not made any crop circles before, but he decided to make some in England. It would be fun to see if people thought a flying saucer had landed. His joke worked. People went wild. For over twelve years, Doug's group of circle-makers fooled many people. There may be lots more jokers out there today.

CEREAL SIGNS

In July 2002 circle-makers made a huge crop design for Weetabix. It took three men several days to 'map out' the design and a total of 16 hours to finish it. 'It must be the most difficult we have ever been asked to make,' they said.

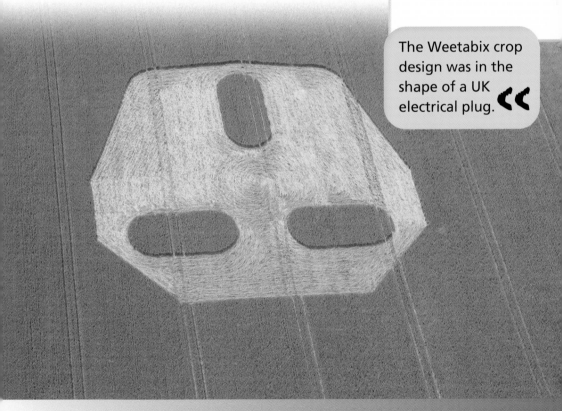

The Weetabix crop design was in the shape of a UK electrical plug. **≪**

remote   far-away place in the middle of nowhere
stake   wooden post with a sharp end for sticking into the ground

SIGNS

Signs is a thriller set in Bucks County, Pennsylvania, USA. Mel Gibson stars as a farmer who discovers crop circles on his farm. He tries to find the truth behind the mysterious circles. There are noises in the night and he sees figures in the moonlight. But that is just the beginning...

ARE WE ALONE?

Crop circles often appear in **UFO** hot spots. People have even reported seeing UFOs hovering over crop circles. But there is still no real proof of this. If **aliens** make crop circles, the question is – why are they doing it? There are three ideas.

- The circles are landing sites for alien spacecraft. 'Flying saucers' flatten the crops where they land.
- The patterns are messages from aliens. They may be a way of saying 'hello' or a warning in code.
- The markings are maps and signs that are made and used by aliens. They may help aliens to find their way or to signal to other aliens.

This bird formation appeared in a field in Wiltshire, in the UK.

business   way of making money
UFO   Unidentified Flying Object

STRANGE SIGNS IN UTAH

In 1996, Seth Alder was about to harvest his wheat in Utah when his tractor broke down. It was then he saw a strange shape cut into his field. There was no sign of anyone having walked in the field. No wheat was broken or stepped on. Then strange lights appeared above the circle at night. It was thought this was the first recorded crop circle light in the USA.

Many thought it was the work of UFOs, which are said to make tractors, cameras or mobile phones stop working. Farm animals have been noisy and nervous on nights when crop circles form nearby.

A PLACE TO STAY

Would you believe that crop circles can make a good love story? The 2002 film *A Place to Stay* was made in Wiltshire, England. The two main characters in the film meet because they both like finding new crop circles.

The subject of 'crop signs' is now good **business** for cinemas. ❱❱

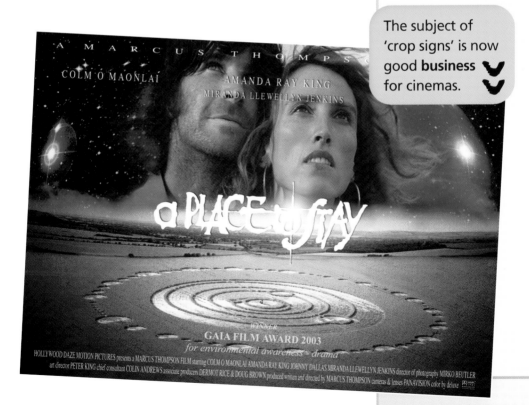

13

CARVED ON THE EARTH

PERU'S SCRATCHPAD

The Nazca plain is very dry and flat. With no sand to cover the plain and little rain or wind, lines drawn in the ground do not rub away. It is like a huge writing pad for artists who wanted to leave their mark for ever.

There are strange lines in the desert of Peru in South America. They are scratched in the ground at Nazca. But it was not until people looked down from aircraft that we knew about these markings. About 300 designs can only be seen properly from the air. They make huge pictures of animals, birds, fish and insects. Some of the animal drawings are more than two football fields long. The big mystery is – why are they there? The markings may be 1500 years old. No one really knows how or why they were made.

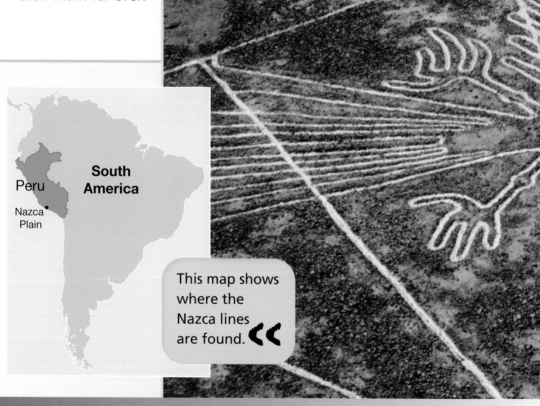

South America

Peru

Nazca Plain

This map shows where the Nazca lines are found. ««

THE ARTISTS

Nazca Indians may have made the Nazca lines. They lived in the area between 300 BC and AD 800. Their pottery has been found around the lines. We know very little about these people and why they would want to draw such lines and shapes. In total there are about 1300 kilometres (800 miles) of straight lines. Some are very narrow and others are hundreds of metres wide. There are triangles, zigzags and spirals. But most amazing are the drawings of a great spider, a monkey and a whale. And the humming bird must be the biggest picture there is of the smallest bird in the world.

The Nazca spider is 45 metres wide!

THE PUZZLE

Since the Nazca lines were found 80 years ago, many scientists have tried to study their meaning. One of them was Maria Reiche, who spent over 50 years studying the drawings. She said, 'We will never know all the answers. That is what a good mystery is all about.'

Whoever created the Nazca lines drew many of the animals around them. This is a humming bird.

WHO IS IT?

In 1982 another drawing was found at Nazca. It is a huge man, 32 metres long. It is often called The Astronaut. Is it an alien? Maybe it is an image of a god. Whatever it is, was it drawn as a sign to something 'up there'?

SIGNS TO SPACECRAFT?

The signs in the Nazca desert raise two big questions. As the lines need to be seen from the sky, did the Nazca Indians know how to fly? Or did they draw their huge pictures for **UFOs**? One mystery has never been solved. Did **ancient** people know how to make and fly hot-air balloons? Pottery found in Peru shows **images** of what may have been balloons or kites. There are also what seem to be burn marks in the desert. These blackened rocks at the end of the lines may have been the **launch sites** for hot-air balloons. Or were they the landing sites of UFOs? We may never know.

This Nazca marking is called the Astronaut. It is probably a drawing of a human or a god.

Key
1 Killer Whale
2 Wing
3 Baby Condor
4 Bird
5 Animal
6 Spiral
7 Lizard
8 Tree
9 Hands
10 Spiral
11 Spider
12 Flower
13 Dog
14 Astronaut
15 Triangle
16 Whale
17 Trapezoids
18 Star
19 Pelican
20 Hummingbird
21 Trapezoid
22 Bird
23 Trapezoid
24 Monkey

WEIRD WORDS   astronomy   study of space and the night sky
baffle   to confuse and mystify

THE GREAT RUNWAY

Some scientists think the lines across the desert are to do with the moon and stars. Perhaps the Nazca Indians drew them to study **astronomy**. But one of the shapes has **baffled** experts for years. It is an arrow-like triangle almost a kilometre long. Some people think it could have been a runway for **alien** spaceships.

Some writers describe the markings as being signs to other aliens. Perhaps 'the runway' was drawn to help others find their way. The shape of the lines is just right for a landing strip.

OTHER SIGNS

The Nazca lines are not the only large drawings scratched on the ground. Others have appeared from California to Chile. But the drawings at Nazca are special. They are so large, with about 300 of them packed into an area of 500 square kilometres (310 square miles).

This map shows some of the main Nazca carvings.

Are the Nazca lines proof that visitors from space came to the Earth years ago?

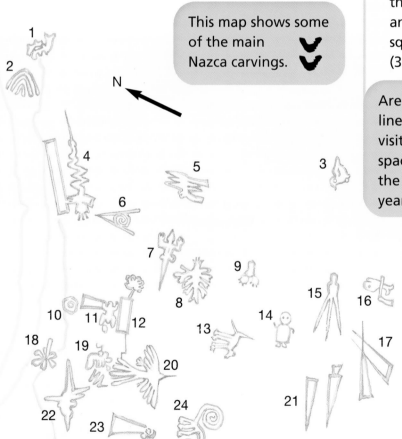

image   drawing or shape made to represent an object
launch site   place where a balloon or flying machine takes off

17

HORSES IN THE HILLS

Is there a link between crop circles and hill carvings? Wiltshire in the UK has many of both. Perhaps ancient people felt a special energy from the Earth here. They may have met in large numbers at their **sacred** white horses to feel the Earth's mystery.

WHITE HORSES

Long ago, people carved shapes into hills. They chose a hill with chalky ground, cut away the grass and turf, and the white chalk underneath showed through. They could make pictures of animals on the hillsides, and the most common shape was a large white horse. There are still many of these horses on English hills, but they are also found all round the world.

SIGNS ON THE HILLS

But why did people make these pictures? Were they trying to signal to someone? Some **ancient tribes** were known to **worship** a horse god. Perhaps these signs on the hills were simply to please the gods.

White horses have been carved onto chalky ground around ❯❯ the world.

fertility   ability to give birth
tribe   group of people with the same beliefs

SHROUDED IN MYSTERY

The White Horse of Uffington near Oxford in England is one of the oldest shapes carved into hills. Scientists think it could be 3000 years old. Its design is different to all others. It is 110 metres long – much larger than other hill markings. It can be seen clearly from 32 kilometres (20 miles) away or from the sky.

There is still much mystery about this white horse. No one knows why it was made all those years ago. Did a local tribe cut it out of the soil as a way to signal to others? Some chalk figures may have been used for magic or as signs to bring **fertility**.

THE WHITE HORSE OF CHIHUAHUA

There is not much mystery about this modern horse on a Mexican mountain. It is a huge copy of the Uffington horse that faces to the left instead of to the right. It is over 0.75 kilometres (0.3 miles) long. It was painted in **whitewash** over 3 years, by Hector Acosta.

The Osmington white horse in the UK is the only one to have a rider. It was made in 1808.

whitewash   white paint made of chalk and water
worship   religious service or ceremony

GIANTS IN THE DUST

The largest human figure at Blythe is 57 metres from head to toe. It has some sort of animal nearby. But what is it telling us? The drawings are now fenced in to stop further spoiling by tyres or feet.

We cannot explain why ancient peoples carved giant human figures onto the Earth.

SECRETS OF THE PAST

In 1931, a pilot flying along the Colorado River in the USA saw giant drawings on the desert floor near Blythe, California. The **images** were faint but one of the figures was about 60 metres long. Since then, over 600 drawings have been found across south-west USA and Mexico.

SIGNS ON THE PLAINS

The drawings are called the Blythe **Intaglio** (pronounced *in tal yoe*). Intaglio means 'a carving'. No one knows who made these carvings in the ground. They may be 200 or 10,000 years old and they show patterns, people and animals. Although many have survived wind and rain, others have been destroyed. Motorbikes, quad bikes and tanks churning up the ground have not helped.

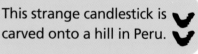

This strange candlestick is carved onto a hill in Peru.

ancestor   people from the past from whom someone has descended

RIDDLES

There are Native Americans living along the Colorado River. Perhaps their **ancestors** made these signs on the plains. Mohave Indians could have made them. Yet present day Mohave do not think this is so.

Perhaps the drawings are messages to **ancient** people's gods or ancestors. Or maybe the pictures tell stories – like a giant comic book. These earth drawings remain a mystery. But just as one pilot found the Blythe Intaglio over 70 years ago, many more may still be waiting to be spotted from the air. And we will never know how many have already been dug up and lost forever.

FISHERMAN

In the foothills of the Plomosa Mountains in the USA is a drawing called The Bouse Fisherman. He has a spear and two fish below him, and a sun and a snake above him. He is very hard to spot and a long way from any water.

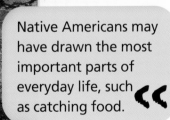

Native Americans may have drawn the most important parts of everyday life, such as catching food. ❝

foothills low hills around the base of a mountain

intaglio engraved image or carving in the rock

21

SECRETS OF THE STONES

THE MYSTERY

Stonehenge is an ancient **monument** on Salisbury Plain. There are many ideas suggesting what it was for.

- Was it a place of **worship** – like a church?
- Was it a place to study the sun and **astronomy**?

Was Stonehenge a **UFO** landing site?

One of the most mysterious places on Earth is Stonehenge in the south-west of England. Once more, the county of Wiltshire is the home to strange energy. The mystery is not just in why, how and when the great slabs of stone were put together. It is also about the feelings that some people have in this area. Many report feelings of strange powers.

STONE CIRCLES

Stone circles were built thousands of years ago. Many of the remains can be found in the UK, Ireland and France. But Stonehenge is different. This ring of great slabs has not been too damaged by time. It is still a place of power and mystery.

Druid   ancient religion of Celtic Britain
monument   old building or structure built for a reason

WONDER

Around 4000 years ago, the stones were brought to the site. Slabs weighing 25 tonnes came from 32 kilometres (20 miles) away. It would have been a major **project** to get them there. How did **ancient** people do it? Experts think they must have dragged them on wooden **sledges**. Before the first stone could be moved, a road had to be cleared through a thick forest. It would not have been an easy job. The ring of huge stones was a very special place. It has been a place of mystery and wonder for many centuries and it will always be so.

KEY QUESTIONS

Was this a place of human **sacrifice**? Some people think the **Druids** used Stonehenge as a place to tie a **victim** on to a slab and bring down the knife... It is all very interesting – but in fact there is little to link the early Druids to Stonehenge.

Each huge stone is about 6 metres tall. ➤➤

project   long-term plan or scheme
sacrifice   killing of an animal or person as an offering

FRENCH SIGNS

The Carnac area of France has many large stones in lines and circles. Several are over 6 metres high. Some rows are over a kilometre long and the stones may be 6000 years old. They may have been **signposts** or graves, for magic or for **astronomy**.

MYSTERY HILL

Forty miles north of Boston, USA, is one of the oldest puzzles of North America. Mystery Hill is also known as 'America's Stonehenge'. It looks very different from the English one, but it may have been built around the same time. It may also have been used for **worship** and as an **observatory** to look at the stars and planets.

Running across the hillside are low walls and cave-like tunnels. There is a huge flat stone like a large table. Many people think this was the **sacrifice** table. A **gutter** round the edge may have been for draining the **victim's** blood away. But who used this place? The mystery remains.

gutter   groove or trough for draining away liquid
myth   made-up tale, told over the years and handed on

STONE CIRCLES

Not far from England's Stonehenge is the mysterious Avebury stone circle. It is the largest stone circle in the world, measuring 427 metres across the middle. The bank and ditch surrounding the stones are more than a kilometre all the way around.

Huge 40-tonne slabs were taken there from a few kilometres away. The ring of stones now has 98 slabs, as some were broken up and used for building a few hundred years ago. But this was always a special place. There are many riddles as to how and why it was built. It was clearly a major meeting place. Even today, some people feel a power here – especially after dark.

AVEBURY

Six hundred years ago some of the stones were moved and one fell on a man. His crushed skeleton was found lying on some scissors, so the stone is now called the Barber's Stone. Another stone is the Devil's Chair. Local **myth** says if you run round it 100 times, you call up the devil.

The Devil's Chair is the most famous Avebury stone.

The Avebury stone circle is the largest in the world.

A SUDDEN END

Over 1000 statues were made from a volcano on Easter Island. Then they were somehow moved up to 22 kilometres (14 miles) away. The great **project** was almost finished and the thousands of islanders were going from strength to strength. Then something went terribly wrong …

EASTER ISLAND MYSTERY

Easter Island has been called the most **remote** spot on Earth. It is in the South Pacific, thousands of kilometres from any **mainland**. The Dutch discovered it in 1722, on Easter Sunday. But its real mystery is the original island people and what they left behind. Around 1500 years ago, the island was a **thriving** place. Its people carved hundreds of giant statues from the rock. Somehow the people moved these stone carvings across the island to where they now stand above the beaches. But the statues did not guard the people very well. Most of the islanders were going to die.

mainland   large area of land or continent
thrive   to grow with strength and do very well

TRAGIC

The giant statues were never finished. **Tribes** on the island began to fight each other. Then in 1862, a slave ship took most of the islanders away to Peru. A few returned and brought back the disease smallpox. The original islanders were nearly wiped out. There was no one left who could read the strange writing carved on the slabs. They remain unread today. Perhaps the writing answers many of the mysteries of the island. Where did its first people come from? Why did they carve the statues? How did they shape and move them? Only the statues themselves know, as they still look out across this tragic island.

MOAI

It is unclear why the Easter Islanders made the statues on such a massive scale. The carved stone heads are called moai and for some reason none looks out to sea. They make an almost unbroken line along the coast of Easter Island.

Some of the moai weigh over 30 tonnes and are 7 metres tall.

THE MEANING OF THE ROUND STONES

The mystery stone balls left many questions behind.

- Were they part of a big model of the stars and planets?
- Were they left from a lost city?
- Were they rolled there as some kind of **ceremony** or sport?

ROLLING STONES

In the 1930s, the jungle was being cleared in Costa Rica in Central America. People found thousands of stone balls buried in the jungle undergrowth. The stone balls were made of granite, which was not naturally found in this area. Were the stones rolled there? The stones were all kinds of sizes.

Each stone was carved into a perfect ball. So where did they come from? Who made them and why? They are yet another mystery from the past. They are likely to be thousands of years old, but no one knows why they were just scattered deep in the thick jungle.

Some of the stones were as big as three metres across and weighed 30 tonnes.

ceremony　special public or religious event
playa　flat dried-up plain in a desert

DEATH VALLEY STONES

In California, USA there are dried-up lakebeds that are now just flat stretches of clay. But strange things happen on the lakebeds when no one is looking. Huge stones move across them. They leave tracks across the dry mud. But the big question is why? Is someone trying to tell us something?

Boulders that weigh over 300 kilograms do not usually slide on their own. There are no slippery slopes on these desert plains. Some scientists think the wind can blow the rocks. Perhaps rain makes the mud very slippery or maybe the rocks slip on ice. But this part of the world rarely sees water or ice. So what is going on?

THE RACETRACK PLAYA

Death Valley in the USA has less than 5 centimetres of rain a year. The ground can reach 57 °C. That is very hot and dry. The dried-up lakes are called **playas**. It is the Racetrack Playa where the mysterious sliding boulders are found.

Are these boulders really moving on their own? ≪

29

POWER OF THE PYRAMIDS

SECRET OF THE SPHINX

A huge stone statue of a sphinx guards the pyramids. A sphinx has a human head and the body of a lion. The age of the Sphinx is a mystery. Wind and water have eaten it away. Some experts think it could be more than 4500 years old.

The **pyramids** of Egypt continue to have a special magic 4500 years after they were built. These huge **monuments** have amazed people down the ages. They are full of wonder and mystery. Despite their age there are still plenty of questions about the pyramids that remain unanswered. There also seem to be darker secrets to uncover and there are stories of curses. These huge signs in the desert will always make our imaginations go wild.

Fast fact

The pyramids were built as burial tombs for ancient Egyptian kings and queens. They believed they took everything with them to an afterlife when they died. That is why their riches were buried with them.

This huge statue guards the pyramids in Egypt. **‹‹**

WEIRD WORDS   afterlife   life after death
burial tomb   sealed room where dead bodies were buried

WHERE DID THE SKILL COME FROM?

Robbers have ripped out the treasures from the pyramids over the years. The tunnels, chambers and **vents** are now bare. But the design of the pyramids remains a work of **genius**. Yet that is not all. They were built in such a way that they line up with certain stars and planets. Who worked out all the maths? Did ancient Egyptians have better skills than us? Did they have help from somewhere? We will never be sure of the answers. Everyone who looks up at the three pyramids at Giza and their millions of blocks of stone must ask the same question. How on earth did they do it?

INSIDE

The Egyptians thought of everything. They knew thieves would be a problem. That is why there are mazes of dark passages, dead ends and hidden rooms inside the pyramids. Burial chambers were sealed with huge granite blocks ... and maybe the odd curse.

genius   amazing mind of extraordinary skill, ability and power
vent   narrow chimney to help air circulation

MIND-BOGGLING

The Great Pyramid is as high as a 42-storey building. It was made from two and a half million stone slabs, without the aid of **precise** tools for measuring or cutting. That took some doing.

HIDDEN MEANINGS

There is far more to the three **pyramids** of Giza than meets the eye. Before raiders stripped the smooth outer stone from these pyramids, they would have looked even more stunning. The white limestone casing was taken away for buildings in Cairo, the capital of Egypt.

At first sight the three pyramids seem to be built in no special order. The writer Robert Bauval discovered that their pattern was an exact match to the stars in **Orion's belt**. These stars were **sacred** to the Egyptians. The **vent** in the top of the Great Pyramid was lined up with the Orion **constellation** – maybe to let the dead king's soul fly up to its resting place in the heavens.

It would have taken over 20,000 workers to build the pyramids. But there is no trace of their living area!

constellation   group of stars
Orion's belt   three bright stars in a short line

THE GREAT PYRAMID

Some people find it hard to believe that the Egyptians built the pyramids just with armies of slaves. It would have taken many years. In fact, some say we could not build the pyramids today, even with modern machines. Will any of today's buildings last for thousands of years?

Whoever built the Great Pyramid knew the Earth well. They knew maths, science, engineering and **astronomy**. The Great Pyramid's position was **vital**. For some reason the builders wanted to leave something behind to last for ever. Maybe the pyramids were just a sign to show how clever the builders were. If so, it worked – for the world is still in wonder.

The Great Pyramid lies at the centre of a world map. Can it just be chance?

PRIME SITE

When all the Earth's land is shown on a map, like the one below, the Great Pyramid is at the very centre. The maths needed to put it right there, with its position to the stars, was outstanding. Was it just **coincidence** or was there a super-human brain behind it?

North America

Europe

Asia

Africa

South America

Australia

Key
▲ Great Pyramid

precise   detailed and very accurate
vital   of real importance

33

TUTANKHAMEN

The Egyptian pharaoh had been dead 3200 years when his body was found. His gold was all around him. But his coffin may well have been the biggest solid gold object ever made. It weighed over 1100 kilograms.

Tutankhamen's burial mask with a **cobra** on its head was gold.

MYTHS AND MAGIC

Many strange stories spread about the **pyramids** of Egypt. Not only are the **monuments** themselves very special, but also what was inside: treasure and **mummies**. What more do you need for a good story? The pyramids make a great **backdrop** for adventure and horror films.

CURSES

Myths began to spread as the tombs inside the pyramids were opened up. Strange writing on the walls inside was said to protect the bodies with a curse. 'Those who enter this tomb shall be visited by wings of death' was a warning that bad things would happen to anyone who broke in.

canary   bright yellow songbird
cobra   poisonous snake

THE LEGEND

In 1923, Lord Carnarvon and his team found the tomb of the **pharaoh** Tutankhamen. It was the discovery of the century. A few weeks later, Carnarvon was dead. He died in his hotel in Egypt from a mosquito bite. It was said the lights went out in the town when he died. Back in England, his dog gave a howl and died. Five months later Lord Carnarvon's brother died. The **rumours** grew of the mummy's curse.

When other members of Carnarvon's team died, the newspapers went wild. The curse of Tutankhamen made a great story. In fact, far more was made of the mystery than was really true.

WINGS OF DEATH

Howard Carter was there at the opening of Tutankhamen's tomb. He lived for another 17 years. But his pet **canary** did not. A cobra swallowed the bird on the day the tomb was opened. And what guards the head of Tutankhamen's mask? A gold cobra.

A curse was said to be written inside Tutankhamen's tomb and soon became feared.

The cobra is part of Egyptian legend.

mummy   embalmed body in an Egyptian tomb
pharaoh   Egyptian king

OTHER PYRAMIDS

One of the oldest and largest pyramids in the world is in Tibet – the White Pyramid. It is hidden away in the mountains, even though it is about 300 metres tall. China has over 100 pyramids and many are thought to be older than those in Egypt.

BEYOND EGYPT

Pyramids do not just belong to Egypt. They were built in other parts of the world thousands of years ago. That in itself is a mystery. What made different peoples at different times and in different places build similar **monuments**?

GREAT MINDS THINK ALIKE

Deep in the jungle of Mexico are the mysterious temples and pyramids of the Maya. These amazing people mapped the stars, **invented** a writing system and were masters of maths. They built pyramids as high as a 20-storey building without metal tools – about 2000 years ago. And just like Egypt's pyramids, those of Mexico are lined up with the stars and **solar system**. How amazing is that?

The pyramid at Chichen Itza in Mexico has 365 steps – one for each day of the year. »

invent   to think up and develop

LOST CITY ON THE MOUNTAIN

The Andes Mountains of Peru hide places of mystery. This was the land of the Inca people. They, too, built special temples to study the stars. Monuments like these helped them to plot the Sun in the sky. This was how they made their calendars.

The Inca began to **thrive** 800 years ago and were doing well until the Spanish came to Peru in the 1530s. The Spanish hunted the Inca down and killed them. But they did not find the Inca's special hideout high in the mountains. This was the secret city of Machu Picchu. Its ruins today show a place of great skill and beauty.

CHANCE?

It so happens that the pyramids of Egypt, Mexico and Tibet are in line across the Earth. Is it just chance that they are all at similar lines of **latitude**? Or does it show that pyramids are not just tombs, but **signposts** to points in the sky?

The city of Machu Picchu was not found until 1911.

North America
Mexico
South America
Europe
Africa
Egypt
Asia
Tibet
Australia

The three most famous pyramids in the world line up across the Earth. Is this a sign?

latitude   the distance of a place (in degrees) north or south of the Equator

37

MYSTERY OF THE MOUNDS

SIGNS ON THE HILL

People were not sure what all the bumps on the hill were at Sutton Hoo in Suffolk, England. In 1939 the bumps were dug open. They were buried ships. Anglo-Saxon kings and their treasure were buried inside. They had been there for 1400 years.

Flat land is best for roads and houses. That is why we have always tried to level out all the humps and bumps. So why did people years ago make more bumps on the Earth's surface? What were they up to?

GREAT SERPENT MOUND

The Great Serpent Mound in Adams County, Ohio, USA is a 400-metre-long hill that is shaped like a snake and is about a metre high. Native Americans probably made it between 1000 and 2000 years ago. They had to dig tonnes of earth from the valley below. That is a lot of work to make a sign that can only be seen clearly from the air.

No one really knows what the Great Serpent Mound in Ohio is for.

WEIRD WORDS   burial mound   ancient man-made hill with bodies buried inside

HUMPS

Silbury Hill is yet another mystery in England's crop-circle county, near Avebury. It is said to have a 'powerful energy' around it, but no one knows why the hill is there.

Silbury Hill is the largest man-made mound in Europe. It must have taken 50 years to make. A lot of soil was needed for something nearly 40 metres high and 167 metres across the base. The hill is a perfect circle and could be even older than the **pyramids**. It is probably a **burial mound** linked to **worship** of some kind.

Perhaps Silbury Hill was used as a giant **sundial**.

CAHOKIA MOUNDS, USA

Many Native American burial mounds are found in the USA. The largest group of about 85 mounds is at Cahokia, Illinois. Around AD 1100, about 20,000 Native Americans lived here. One mysterious mound even appears to have something like a stone pyramid inside.

sundial instrument for telling the time by the shadow of a pointer cast by the Sun

MAY THE FORCE BE WITH YOU

The Earth's poles are like giant magnets. They drive unseen currents round the globe. Our upper **atmosphere** is charged with electric particles. Power is all around. Perhaps **dowsers**, who use twigs to find water, tune in to some of these mysterious pulses and signals.

LEY LINES

Some people say they can sense a kind of energy at **ancient** man-made hills or stone **monuments**. Perhaps such places were built on **invisible** lines of mysterious energy that run across the Earth. These lines are often called **ley lines**.

ENERGY CHANNELS

In the 1920s, Alfred Watkins studied maps and old tracks. He noticed that **sacred** sites seemed to be joined by ley lines. Ancient peoples around the world appear to have believed in special lines linking their sacred places. It is as though channels of energy flow across the Earth and meet at 'power points' like Stonehenge. In fact, modern science can sometimes measure energy bursts in these special places.

Dowsers use sticks to detect natural energy.

atmosphere   layer of gases around the Earth

LINES IN THE USA

A lot of study has gone into these special lines in the USA. One of them is called the Hopewell Highway of Ohio. It is said to run from the Great Circle Mound, Newark as a spirit path. This is like a ley line.

Some Native Americans have believed in such sacred trails for centuries. The Hopi of Arizona believe in an Earth spirit. When crop circles appeared thousands of miles away, they said these were the **symbol** of the Earth spirit. So perhaps ancient sites, the Earth's energy and crop circles are all linked. Are they just signs of deeper mysteries we have yet to explore?

ULURU

Uluru, or Ayer's Rock, is a huge mound in central Australia. It has been sacred to the Aboriginal people for centuries. They, too, talk of 'dreaming tracks' that join such sacred places. Sometimes they have followed them to find new places to live, led by the Earth's spirit.

The Great Circle Mound in Newark, the USA, has been made into a golf course. ◀◀

invisible   *cannot be seen*

DINOSAUR VALLEY, TEXAS

Huge beasts left tracks in mud, which then became fossils in solid rock. These are signs that help us understand mysteries of the past. Not long ago we knew nothing about the world of dinosaurs. The rocks are now unlocking their secrets.

SIGNS INSIDE THE STONES

Signs from the past have been left not just on hills but also inside them. Rocks and stones can tell us about our planet thousands of years ago. They can also raise new mysteries.

LOCKED IN THE ROCK

Rocks in the Nevada Canyon in the USA are over 160 million years old. **Fossils** of creatures from that time are locked inside the rock. These creatures lived long before humans ever walked the Earth. Yet in 1927 a print of a human shoe was found in this **ancient** rock. How did it get there? Some say it cannot be a fossil, while others think it is proof that human-like beings once walked this planet long ago.

Signs on the rocks of Dinosaur Valley help scientists learn about these creatures.

How did Egyptian carvings end up in Australia?

WEIRD WORDS fake   not real or a forgery
fossil   remains or print of an animal from long ago

SIGNS ON THE STONES

Australia has a real rock mystery. At Gosford in the Hunter Valley, there are old Egyptian signs carved on two rock walls facing each other in a narrow **gorge**. The rocks are covered in Egyptian-like pictures and **symbols**. People have known about them for 100 years and think the ancient Egyptians drew them thousands of years ago. But the big question is: what were Egyptians doing in Australia? And what were they trying to say? The pictures are nothing like the ancient art of Aboriginal Australians.

Some people think the carvings are **fakes**. But the mystery still remains.

STONE LAUNCH PADS?

Baalbeck is an ancient city in Lebanon. The Romans built huge temples there with the biggest stone slabs ever made. One is about 1000 tonnes and stands at the **quarry**. The mystery is how they were ever moved.

Some people say the slabs were platforms for **alien** spaceships.

gorge   steep and narrow rocky gully
quarry   where stone is cut out of the ground or from a cliff

43

DENTS AND DIMPLES

The Earth's surface is full of strange marks. There are huge holes and dents. For centuries people could only guess how they got there. Recent satellite pictures show their size. Now we can read the signs of how our planet has been attacked over the years.

ASTEROIDS

Sometimes an **asteroid** hits the Earth. An asteroid is a huge mass of rock that orbits the Sun. It is like a small planet that can be up to 965 kilometres (600 miles) across. Luckily only smaller asteroids have hit the Earth so far.

BARRINGER CRATER

The Barringer Crater is a massive hole in the Arizona Desert in the USA. It is nearly 1.5 kilometres (1 mile) wide and 200 metres deep. Its rim is made of smashed rock from inside the crater and rises 50 metres above the plain. Some lumps of rock are the size of houses. Its other name is '**Meteor** Crater', which tells us how it got there.

An asteroid just 300 metres in size could wipe out a whole country if it hit the Earth.

STAR WARS

Huge lumps of ice or rock fall from space. The **impact** on the Earth can be enormous. It may be like hundreds of nuclear bombs going off at once. Some of the bigger craters from millions of years ago show the force that hit the Earth. We have always been under attack from space.

About 120 craters have been **identified** on the Earth. There may be more, but some craters have almost been worn away.

WOLFE CREEK, AUSTRALIA

Wolfe Creek sinks 50 metres below its rim. Like the Barringer Crater, this is just a dimple. And it only happened a few thousand years ago. That is just like yesterday in the Earth's millions of years of existence.

SIGNS FROM SPACE

Satellites can show us the size of past mystery meteor craters.

Sudbury, Ontario, Canada

200 kilometres
(125 miles) across
1850 million years old

Chicxulub, Mexico

170 kilometres
(105 miles) across
65 million years old

Acraman, Australia

160 kilometres
(100 miles) across
570 million years old

The Barringer Crater was formed just a few thousand years ago, when a meteor smashed into the Earth. ❝

meteor   burning matter and dust from outer space

THE MYSTERY OF 1908

Less than a hundred years ago, a huge explosion rocked Russia. People in a **remote** village saw a fireball falling to Earth. Then came a bang and the ground shook. The explosion was heard 800 kilometres (500 miles) away. Smoke poured into the sky. Although some people talked of a crashed **UFO**, this could well have been an ice **meteorite**. That is because no remains were ever found. But no crater was left behind, either. That really was a mystery. But it did leave other mysterious signs behind.

ATTACK

Some people think that the dinosaurs were killed by a giant asteroid millions of years ago. The **asteroid** hit the Earth and exploded. It released gases and dust that blocked out the Sun. Gases from the explosion mixed with rain and made it **poisonous**. All the dinosaurs died.

Whatever shook Tunguska in 1908 must have exploded in the air. Was it an alien spacecraft?

meteorite   large lump of rock, metal or ice from space

SIGNS OF A BOMB

The **impact** area was called Tunguska. It took years for scientists to find the crash site. When they did, they were shocked. A huge forest had been burned and flattened. Thousands of trees had been thrown down like matchsticks in an area that stretched 90 kilometres (55 miles) in a fan shape. This was nothing like the **meteor** crater of Arizona. There was no doubt that great heat and energy had hit the Earth. Also, levels of **radiation** were very high. It was just like the remains of a nuclear explosion. But nuclear bombs would not be made for another 35 years – at least, not on the Earth.

CHICXULUB, YUCATAN PENINSULA, MEXICO

NASA scientists think an asteroid about 16 km (10 miles) across made this crater in Mexico 65 million years ago. The dust from the impact blotted out the Sun for about half a year, and the planet began to freeze.

This computer graphic shows the impact a meteor would have on the Earth. ❯❯

SIGNS ON MARS

Of all the planets, Mars has always been of special interest to us. That is because it is just next door. It is more like the Earth than the other planets in the **solar system**. We used to think **aliens** lived there. We now know otherwise. Or do we? After all, we can see strange things on the surface of Mars that raise questions.

HILLS, CRATERS OR SIGNS OF LIFE?

Some people think the photos of Mars, like the one above, show:

- great pyramids
- a city with a fort
- a ruin on a hill, like Machu Picchu
- a crashed spacecraft
- a row of huge slabs – like Stonehenge.

People used to think the lines that can be seen on Mars were canals or roads. Clearer pictures show that they are more like **gullies**. Perhaps they were made by water. And where there is water there may be life.

NASA hope to put humans on Mars by 2040. Perhaps they will unlock the mysteries of this planet's surface. 》》

civilization   advanced and organized group of people
gullies   deep valleys, canyons or ravines

NEW DISCOVERIES

Space missions to Mars should soon find if there ever was life on Mars. An apple-size **meteorite** from Mars hit Earth long ago. Inside the meteorite scientists found **fossils** of tiny cells. This could be the first sign that there was once life on Mars.

In 1976, **NASA's** Viking mission sent pictures back from Mars. One of them looks like a face. It looks just like the Sphinx of Egypt. And nearby, there seem to be **pyramids**. Many people have studied the photo. They say it cannot be a trick of the light as there is something solid there. It must be 650 metres high and 1.5 kilometres (1 mile) wide. But what is it?

WHAT DO THESE SIGNS MEAN?

- Does the 'sphinx' of Mars prove there was once an alien **civilization** as great as our own?
- Did the builders of the Earth's pyramids have 'contacts' on other planets?

What do you think?

Look carefully at this photo of Mars' surface and you can see a mysterious face. **‹‹**

WHAT ON EARTH WILL WE LOOK LIKE?

FUTURE DANGER?

"

This is a **hazard** we can deal with and we must deal with. And remember, you are much less likely to die in an asteroid **impact** than you are in a car accident.

"

Duncan Steel, Vice President of the Spaceguard Centre, UK.

Our planet is full of secrets and it seems that it always will be. Will we ever understand all the mysteries out there? Just as we solve some of the those that puzzled our **ancestors,** we find more. It is only in the last 100 years that we have been able to fly. Since then, we have uncovered far more mysterious signs from our new bird's-eye view. In the last 50 years of space travel we have found even more puzzles on our planet and beyond. What signs will our age leave behind? Some are already quite worrying.

Just how will tomorrow's space travellers see Earth?

WEIRD WORDS   hazard   danger or risk

THE SCENE FROM ABOVE

Satellite photos already show us what we are doing to our planet.

- The rainforests are disappearing very fast.
- The holes in the **ozone layer** are growing because of pollution.
- The ice caps are melting and sea levels are rising.

But the future need not look too gloomy. We can already see the signs and we know what we have to do. We just need to take care of our planet. A planet that has been handed on to us, with all its secrets from the past. And with all its mysterious energy. Perhaps the 21st century will begin to bring just a few of the answers.

COMING SOON...

An asteroid known as 4179 orbits the Earth. It moves at 40 kilometres (25 miles) per second, getting closer all the time. Some **astronomers** have worked out when it may strike. A news headline recently read:

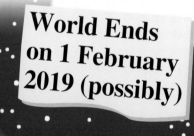

World Ends on 1 February 2019 (possibly)

Our planet is more likely to be destroyed by pollution than an **asteroid** impact.

ozone layer   layer of gas round the Earth that absorbs the Sun's radiation

FIND OUT MORE

WEBSITES

PYRAMIDS
Amazing site with information about the mysteries of Egypt.
pbs.orgwgbh/nova/ pyramid/

CROP CIRCLES
Photos and stories behind crop circles found in Canada.
CropCircleQuest.com

NAZCA LINES
The facts and mysteries behind these huge signs in Peru.
crystalinks.com/nasca. html

STONEHENGE
Read the history of the stones on the official site.
english-heritage.org. uk/stonehenge/

BOOKS

Can Science Solve? The Mystery of Crop Circles, Chris Oxlade and Anita Ganeri (Heinemann Library, 1999)

Can Science Solve? The Mystery of Stone Circles, Paul Mason (Heinemann Library, 2002)

The Unexplained Pack, (Tick Tock, 2003)

WORLD WIDE WEB

If you want to find out more about mysterious signs, you can search the Internet using keywords like these:

- 'mysterious signs'
- crop + circle
- ancient civilizations

You can also find your own keywords by using headings or words from this book. Use the search tips below to help you find the most useful websites.

SEARCH TIPS

There are billions of pages on the Internet so it can be difficult to find exactly what you are looking for. If you just type in 'sign' on a search engine like Google, you will get a list of 88 million web pages. These search skills will help you find useful websites more quickly:

- Know exactly what you want to find out
- Use simple keywords, not whole sentences
- Use two to six keywords in a search
- Be precise – only use names of people, places or things
- If you want to find words that go together, put quote marks around them
- Use the + sign to add certain words, for example typing signs + earth into the search box will help you find web pages related to mysterious markings.

WHERE TO SEARCH

SEARCH ENGINE

A search engine looks through the entire web and lists all the sites that match the words in the search box. The best matches are at the top of the list, on the first page. Try **bbc.co.uk/search**

SEARCH DIRECTORY

A search directory is like a library of websites. You can search by keyword or subject and browse through the different sites like you would look through books on a shelf. A good example is **yahooligans.com**

GLOSSARY

afterlife   life after death

ancestor   people from the past from whom someone has descended

ancient   from a long time ago

asteroid   huge rock that orbits the Sun

astronomy   study of space and the night sky

atmosphere   gases surrounding the Earth

baffle   to confuse and mystify

burial mound   ancient man-made hill with bodies buried inside

burial tomb   sealed room where dead bodies are buried

business   way of making money

ceremony   special event

civilization   advanced and organized group

cobra   poisonous snake

coincidence   when two or more strange things happen at the same time or place

complex   hard or complicated

constellation   group of stars

dowser   someone who uses sticks or rods to find water or minerals

Druid   ancient religion

examine   study something

fertility   ability to give birth

foothills   low hills around the base of a mountain

fossil   remains of an animal from long ago

fraction   small part of the total

genius   amazing mind

gorge   steep and narrow rocky valley

gutter   groove or trough for draining away liquid

hazard   danger or risk

hoax   joke, trick or something that is not real

image   drawing or shape made to represent an object

impact   one body coming into contact with another at speed

intaglio   engraved image or carving in the rock

invent   to think up and develop

invisible   cannot be seen

latitude   the distance of a place (in degrees) north or south of the equator

launch site   where a balloon or flying machine takes off

ley lines   invisible lines that are said to run across the landscape, thought by some to be lines of mysterious energy

magnetic pulling force – attracted by the power of the north and south poles

mainland large area of land

mankind human species over thousands of years

meteor burning matter and dust from outer space

meteorite large lump of rock, metal or ice from outer space

monument old building or structure built for a reason

mummy embalmed body

myth made-up tale, told over the years and handed on

NASA National Aeronautics and Space Administration (the US space organization)

observatory place to observe the planets, stars, Sun and Moon

Orion's belt three bright stars

ozone layer layer of gas around the Earth

pharaoh Egyptian king

playa flat dried-up plain

precise detailed and accurate

project long-term plan or scheme

pyramid large stone monument with sloping sides and a point

quarry where stone is cut out of the ground or from a cliff

radiation invisible waves of energy

reed plants with tall stalks that grow in water

remote far away from people

rumour story based on gossip

sacred special in a religious way

sacrifice killing of an animal or person as an offering

sledge platform that is pulled across the ground

solar system our group of planets that orbit the Sun

stake wooden post with a sharp end for sticking into the ground

sundial instrument for telling the time by the shadow of a pointer cast by the Sun

symbol sign with a meaning

thrive to grow with strength and do very well

tribe group of people with the same beliefs who live closely together

UFO Unidentified Flying Object

vent narrow chimney to help air circulation

victim person who gets hurt or killed

vital really important

whitewash white paint made of chalk and water

worship religious service or ceremony

INDEX